CITIES

CITIES

a poem by
WILLIAM CARNEY

North Atlantic Books
Berkeley, California

Cities

ISBN 0-938190-58-X

Publisher's address:
North Atlantic Books
2320 Blake Street
Berkeley, California 94704

Cover and book design, Paula Morrison
Editorial advice, Mark Livingston
Typeset in Garamond by Classic Typography
Printed in the United States
Cover photograph flown March 27, 1984, by Lockwood Kessler & Bartlett, Inc., Syosset, New York.

The author warmly acknowledges the long support and insightful criticism accorded *Cities* by many friends and by members of the Small Press Traffic writing workshop, which is partially funded by the California Arts Council.

Portions of this poem appeared previously in *Io #33, Nuclear Strategy and the Code of the Warrior.*

The current publication of *Cities* is sponsored in part by the Society for the Study of Native Arts and Sciences, a nonprofit educational corporation.

Library of Congress Cataloging in Publication Data

Carney, William, 1948-
    Cities.

    I. Title.
PS3553.A7583C5   1985   811'.54   85-7132
ISBN 0-938190-58-X

For my parents

PREFACE

This poem portrays an ordinary day in the late twentieth century, that is, a day on which everything may end. The portrait is in twelve parts, each rendering the day in terms of a different character, setting, hour, situation, rhetoric and perspective. Though multiple and inconclusive, the shifting parts are held together by the gravity of their single point in time and by the connection (I believe) of all people and all things on a single, lonely, lovely planet.

It is in fact the outlines of an earthwide polis which *Cities* seeks to discern against the shadow of impending nucleoclysm. If it is to last, the piles of such an earthly city must be driven deep. Its foundations must reach, as does Section 3 of the poem, toward a comprehension of war's hellish history and capacity. They must touch psychological and evolutionary roots, as Sections 4 and 5 attempt. They must rest on the bedrock of human love in various phases—at conception (Section 7), at death (Section 8), and at the struggling emergences of childhood (Section 10). And sadly, such foundations must take into account—as Sections 6 and 9 endeavor—the sloppy, harrowing, small-minded and mean-hearted violence of which culture is capable.

In working on the poem, I pictured sometimes the role of language in an early human hunt. Each hunter holds in mind a somewhat different image of the shifting herd. The cooperation of the hunters—and thereby the success of the hunt—

depends on the communication through language of a single 'all points' image throughout the group. Again, now, our ability as individuals to frame accurate world views and to communicate these to the larger human group may see us through to punctuated but nonetheless continuing sustenance.

William Carney

1

*It is morning on an autumn day in an American city. The subject
of the poem—the pending nuclear destruction of the earth—is first
depicted as a man on the verge of suicide. He struggles to comprehend
the dizzying dimensions of his situation. A last-ditch gleam of sense
comes as he imagines himself photographing the city during the fall
to his death. It is a city steeped in destructiveness; war is brewing,
the economy's sour, loneliness and random violence pervade. There
are also pigeons, music and human kindness. He commits himself
to document this world.*

The man stands in a high place, city
mapped below. His footing is cliché.
He does not know why he is there.
He studies morning air, attempting
to recall. He will decide now not
just futures, but his past. Honking street
jazz rises, sirens rushing like pitched
water all directions warnings. Sound
coils like a python. Hand grips
plaster, buttresses and spires once
heroic. *Give me strength*, he asks
the air. Pigeons in a whirlwind
detonate behind him. He looks down.
Slowly at first then gaining speed whole
buildings lift like missiles toward the sky.

Wind holds him sane.

                        He steps back, breathes
deeply as a swimmer might, takes out
deliberately a camera, sets
aperture, exposure, power drive,
secures round neck,

                 smiling

                         to think how
they'd blow it up, every last detail
pinned against the wall, headquarters
crazy to put back together
the exact event: what failure of
what hinted anger, love, ambition,
fear.

      They close in magnifying each
constituent of frozen light, then
back off like men discovering some
mammoth glacial carcass, straining for
some sense of the totality:

                       odd
angled building fragments shot perspectives
all diverging.

          pigeons stopped

                     midflight
torquing like mad.

            sidewalk crap game
die cast over and again—*them bones
is good now, hit me*—people knotted
all hopes riding on the roll of these
numbered geometries.

and corner
after corner newsstand 60 pt.
moderna bold

BIG WAR BUILDUP

god
help us picture inside picture men
diminishing, keelless craft ascrape on
bottom sands innumerable.

inside
the briefcase, man, inside. what, angel
dust? come on. the fucker blow up in
your face, you staring at it, dumb.

random
notes of symphony violinist out
of work, she plays bus stops and movie
lines, the places people wait.

not bad.

how else she make it out

that hellhole?

still don't speak

the language.

milling
pigeons, wide-eyed, commonplace, clumsy
and iridescent, some hovering
tumultuous as ocean pushed
this way and that, confused, all scrambling
for grain the silver lady of
the dumpster spreads about her.

and on and
on stray arguments.

so what's for sure.
you liquidate the sucker. anytime
before maturity.

dialect. you
got to understand the dialectic
subtleties. the world is going to be
the way I say.

man crumpled at
the door, blood safely deposited,
lifts once more the empty, clarion
against white lips.

and answering sweet
sirens sing and everyone looks up,
drawn in, a moment's unity and
recognition.

It's then the man resolves
to do high duty to an autumn
day, to document his fall, the way
a pilot to provide intelligence
will ride his sacrificial solo
jet thin-winged through high thin air to capture
changes back behind the lines. Or like
the thing itself, a bomb whistling
headlong to utter ruination—
terrorists hold it, making their demands
in full floodlight, *freedom absolute,*
love guaranteed—with such free-fall
intensity, the grainy concrete now
uprushing actuality, he sings.

2

The metaphor shifts from suicide to accident as a woman recounts some of the circumstances surrounding the death of her former lover in a car wreck the preceding night. Again the event is hard to understand. It may be the result of a simple addiction to technology—the technology of freedom, loose and autonomous—coupled with the simple randomness of things. It may indicate a momentary breakdown in the casual, communal responsibility of the road. Lingering about, however, is the smell of broken trust, broken relationship, unformed commitment. We learn that the brewing war has something to do with oil.

He dropped me off at twelve o'clock.
The rain dropped steadily all night.
The traffic ran red taillights. I don't know.
We talked a lot. He was so glad
about the rain, kept saying how now
everything would grow. Silly in the fall.
He had that kind of cosmic take on things,
the whole year at a time. The water
would soak down, get in among the roots, freeze,
then thaw, eventually. *Dendritic
grows reality.* He talked like that.
The road is just the belly of the snake.
He loved to drive. The highways seemed to know.
He'd take a curve and concentrate it

down to something he could hold there in
his hand. Imagine miles of landscape
held like that, caressed. I'd feel so sexual
on a long trip, sometimes we'd have to
stop. Cars do that to some women.
We were well matched, I guess. He'd touch me
easy till I came, a half an hour
maybe, driving deep into the night,
the country hills and fragrances
the only other presence felt. The man
could drive. I don't know how this happened.
He dropped me off at twelve o'clock.
We were stone sober. We'd broken up
a month ago. Last night we did
an excellent job of being friends.
We were recovering. He wanted
to go home to work on something. Strange
man, he said, *Rush hour when the freeway's*
stalled, I miss you most. Nights he could handle.
He felt alone at night he'd get back
in the car and drive at random
all around the city. *Nights,* he said
the motor stretches like a cat. Goddamn
machine. Goddamn man. He was too proud
to stay. *Elementary physics, no*
two objects. He talked like that, defending
all the time what is it men find so
important? I don't know. Everybody
drives these fucking missiles down the street,
through neighborhoods, into the heart
of cities, anyplace they want, just
blindly trusting nothing's going to happen
one more day. It's how we stay alive.
It's what he knew of grace and beauty.
You don't think anymore about it

than about your blood cells operating
how they're supposed to. Then someone misses
one cup of coffee. Or has an extra
drink. Or steers a little to the music.
Or maybe there's no cause at all, but things
go wrong. And suddenly it's over.
The motion stops. The soft flesh hurtling
through air comes up hard against metal
and glass, concrete, that whole encompassing
world turned deadly. *Suspended*
animation, he would call it. Now
I'm the one that's numbed. You'd think nothing
had happened. It's how we stay alive.
He'd been hit once before, you know,
rear-ended out of nowhere. His teeth
caught the steering wheel. They strung him back
together—*like some fossil jaw pulled*
from the gorge at Olduvai, he said—
the dentist all the time explaining
how when aliens extract us from
the rubble, modern dentistry would seem
earth's crowning work of evolution.
For weeks he shyed from traffic, painfully
aware, like someone mugged or raped,
how vulnerable our trusting is. Hurt
people will antenna pain. He felt
it in his teeth, November days, each
fallible creak of brakes, cracked asphalt
surface, the violence of steel flung
through air. He felt his teeth against his gums
like stone, a hardness in him gritted
up against the possibility
of pavement, flesh tenuous at best.
That fall we stopped to help out at a wreck.
The moans, everything existed in

this awful pool of silence. It was like
half-way through a movie someone drops
the projector on the audience.
There was nothing we could do. We were
strangers waiting for sirens. I cut
off a car radio. *Asphaltic*
subgrade hadn't been compacted right.
He got real sick later that night, then
told me how in small towns in the South
his cousins and their friends for lack
of anything to do would cruise from town
to town the long black reaches of tar
road slicing through tall pinewoods, flat black fields
until, as certain as roulette, one missed
a curve. Such deaths are discussed for years.
Last night we talked about this oil mess
and general politics, nothing more
gothic. He'd been experimenting
with raku. He said the firing's
a process of great subtlety and
violence. It has to happen fast.
He painted dragonflies on every vase.
Still, the wheel was his chief pleasure,
lifting centered earth toward symmetry
that he could feel there in his fingers.
He liked a grainy photograph and jazz
a little husky. He liked a final
note sustained as long as possible.

3

*A reporter arrives at a military base for an early morning tour down
a missile silo. His fragmented notes eventually take the form of a
countdown, chronicling war's history. The descent is into hell; all
history seems the arsenal. At the pentultimate circle—the nuclear
circle, the circle of silence—the diminishing countdown expands back
out in the familiar bullseye rings of nuclear destruction.*

You get there along roads that section
land, a minute at a time, precise square
miles of corn, wheat, barley, sunflowers
surging softly as the ocean once
rode this terrain. How these geometries
amaze: grid tightens eastward into
cities, taproot to transmitting
kernel, your own mind recollecting
diatoms of all dimensions settling,
soft flakes of light, into eventual
stone: this gathering, this memory
the foundation of wide harvests,
limestone buildings and crushed gravel roads.
It's dawn. From the horizon rise
cylindric silos. The rhythm now
picks up phone poles, flashing, then the swoop
of wires like a goldfinch in between
communicating town to town,

quick exclamations adding up to
one plain statement at the core of each
community: grain nucleus,
acropolis of grain stored up from
intervening countryside.

Now grid
again the air, imposing chain link
strands as if this bounded land were tilted
up, abstracted, punched through like a sieve.
You hold this to your eyes. Prepare
credentials.

Stop.

NOTES.   U.S. NUCLEAR
PREPAREDNESS.

Voltaire, North Dakota.
the readiness is all.

invert now
imagery of aspiration. draw
horizon in. dark circle sunk
against pitched plains.

a sun collapsed on
cindered self bores down through time a hole
like this, worlds reeling into it.

you
spiral down steel staircase,

missile hung
like pupa waiting,

round and round, thick
woven silence deadening approach.

                          as
cranes once thunderous brought down this sky,
lines

        untangled, recombined,

                          now twisting
toward mute vanishment.

                    as spider
dizzying spins out itself.

                    as bats
return clockwise to a dark place.

                          as
snow, warped cyclops storm, blind whiteout through which
men will circle till they drop.

                    air, bear
this weight.

                the way hear tell a man once
hung legs churning over tidal
vortex, strange waters he had ventured
in,

        now grasping his last hope these straining
roots hands chanced upon.

                          you're losing it.
mirrored metal wall bangs back and forth
the image and reality,
beautiful distortions

                    like the deer
antelope and mammoth figuring
forgotten magics

of fecundity
and kill.

you turn to place palms flat on
wall, search seam or crevice, fly-like, to get
hold of.

breath registers on the surface,
disappears, your own face

comes and goes
then others knotted, dense-packed, struggling
conglomerate flesh

mouthing to break through
to you.

and at your back, hissing
escaping oxygen, far down slow
roar begins

as in incoming shells
the ocean curls.

NINE.

fire flickering.

just natural. we've always been this way.

the cave piled up with calcium.

the way
kids take to a computer game.

as if
long gone from off the earth, huge bear shagged
as oak wood prominence, uprushes
from the cave's throat scattering

trapped men

like leaves in front of winter

> brushing
them aside, gray cortex splattered on
gray stone.

EIGHT.

> Agamennon had it.

gets me right here in the gut sometimes
deep down.

> the hollow horns.

> proud bronze
projectile enters at the cheek, just
under left eye, crashing through clenched teeth and
out part way the neck

> miraculously
severing

> neither trachea nor
spinal cord. he falls

> still breathing
and aware.

> they found at Troy forty
circling cities (where now uncounted
grasses pulse again)

> naming them
horizons.

SEVEN.

> *walking down*

the goddamn street. WHAM. *anytime
your number's up.*

set stone to stone.

take

charcoal, saltpeter, sulfur.

swallow

hard

(the black spore bursting into life)

feel

inside the cell

walls permeable

Constantinople

the explosion

inside

out

cells screaming separations

as a jet

end over end

down

city canyons.

this prime equation.

1453. *no stopping it.*

SIX.

just have to hold our own.

two years

before Plymouth, eleven after

Jamestown,

        similarly an expression
of spiritual fragmentation,
secular expansion,

        an exploding
world.

    this nation born of.

        and numbers:
30 Years War.   7,000,000 Dead
War.

    and most of these civilians.

        caught
up in

    slush and sleet they cannot
move

    for malnutrition, skeletal
or (sure sign) stomachs full

        of air or
corpses bloated, wide-eyed, quiet. as
maggots in a mass grave

        writhing fruit
drink red.

    numb numbers.

        fattened at
the same trough all of us.

        Westphalia
1648, pieced Europe
into states, each granted rights to war
and taxes.

temporal sovereignty.

the human rule

of space and time.

FIVE.

take your average individual
lying low,

bogged down, scared

stiff, you stick
a flag up

over him (whips furious)
he'll fight like hell

anything to keep
the feeling strong.

the isolated
shots ring out, one by one, one following
another.

got to stand up sometime
and be counted.

sweat crawls over you like
insects.

take the American
Revolution, guerillas, freedom
over all else,

every man his own war.

take French liberty, imposing
compulsory military service
to salvage revolution.

take Prussia
which organized a) peacetime conscription;
b) war is politics; c) war is all
out, a romantic construct

(look
again at Delacroix and Wagner):

Lorraine won in six weeks.

breathtaking.

take the lone man,

seventeen, blondish
hair, slight wave cut smartly over
forehead, knowing and uncertain eyes
alive

as told all out the hundred yards
against machinery

flashing *brighter*
than a thousand suns.

FOUR.

as lit
apartments or entire city
burning cold with them

wide fields of stone
return the dying sun.

unlid the grave,
the warm life under each flames out.

count each:

gallipoli: two hundred
thirteen thousand nine hundred eighty.

antietam: 22,000.

   mukden:
160,000.

   verdun:
330,000.

   the somme:
1,000,000.

    stalingrad: 2,000,000.

korea: 5,000,000.

   first world war total:
40,000,000 dead.

   second world war:
60,000,000 dead.

           numb numbers. cold.

what is incomprehensible must be
experienced.

         crossed soldiers, gift-tied, sent
away.

    ticking half-lives massed.

                THREE.

dachau	sachsenhausen	*buchenwald*
mathausen	flossenburg	ravensbruck
auschwitz	neuengamme	gusen
natzweiler	*gros rosen*	lublin
niederhagen	stutthof	arbeitsdorf

TWO.

 hamburg

 stuttgart

 dresden

 guernica

berlin

 cologne

 dusseldorf

 london

coventry

 tokyo

 perfect

release:

 distant,

 casual

 as rain, these
hard accumulations,

 end over
end

 through pliant air,

 reptilian,
descend,

 soft constrictions of cold breath
left rising from

 the surfaces of things.

snake must got his tongue.

hiroshima.

nagasaki.

ONE.

hear now this.

mycelia of silence

spreading
through you, covering

your surfaces
the way clouds mildew earth.

the way men
strain in silence nearing laboratory
breakthrough

(and the world waits quietly
for word).

*nothing we can do nothing
nothing.*

the way in institutions
persons piecemeal feed out mind, thin line
sunk against

tumultuous silence
nothing answering, reel and chum much
as they may.

you know what's next, how

two mile circle. gamma radiation
kills outright. cells droop like Dali clocks.

how eight mile circle. 400 mile per
hour wind avalanches buildings,
transforms everything to missile.
people driven as nails or blind snow.

how ten mile circle. fireball blinds
anyone caught looking. flesh cooks, laced
by its surroundings. this page ignites.

how thirty mile circle. burning dark
snow descends, *protracted afterburst*,
a trillion hiroshimas in the cells
of anyone exposed. each person
in decay, internally, in merger
with their own echoing creation.

how circles of indefinite
diameter. electromagnetic pulse
kills all communication.

how interpenetrating circles.
multiply. one megaton by
seven thousand megaton attack
to fifteen thousand megaton
mutual exchange, a *saturation
bombing* of two continents, towns down
to fifteen hundred (Housatonic,
Bethel, Cloverdale). *local effects*
like pebbles in a pond, each city
grown to join with all others
in a wash of fire, radiation, shock.

how circles of worldwide necropolis.
from carcasses of mammals, carcass
hills, the seepage into oceans
starts, and exponentially

the populations of bacteria
bloom cyclic waves *ad nauseum*.

how atmospheric circles, circles
of air. the dust from this fight rises, spreads
radiation earthwide strong enough
to mutate who knows what future
generations. blocks significant
sunlight cooling (maybe trapping, heating
up) till climates, ice floes, oceans
also mutate. finally recombinant
with ozone, depleting seventy
percent, allows in ultraviolet
sunlight now becomes the blinding flash
steadily intense for thirty years
on all surviving grain and retinas.

ZERO.

        Feel then one last time your
fingers on the missile's skin, sweating
condensation cold the way antarctic
metal sticks to you, burning, stripping
flesh away: reach now toward this
absolute, all motion stopped: inside
hungry for your touch, the tonguing fire
roars into awareness lifting every
language skyward: ride, ride this high craft
clean out into empty apogee
then turn—the earth suspended past belief
beautiful and brief—then hurtle home.

4

The descent continues, interior now, in a dream told to a psychologist. The analysis which follows conducts the dreamer deeper into the realms of his own violence.

A crab or crayfish backs away from
two huge presences. An overgrown
claw holds each at bay, opening
and closing like the mouths of fledgling
birds. Nothing comes out. An octopus
sulks on the right, soft, its tentacles
suckered with teats. These secrete black ink
through which, obscurely, one can see
the looming naked head, cow eyes, and
beak, slowly working. To the left
a phallic shark is circling, its
leather skin and scale teeth guided by
a brain that's mostly optics. The dead clear
water through which it moves is laced with blood.
Both close on the retreating crab. Then
behind it, the crustacean senses
new danger: a soft glow emitted
from a lamp dropped centuries ago
to the ocean floor. There is no choice.
It backs into the lamp. On impact
crab begins to grow so fast its shell

splits, sweet innards dangerously exposed.
It drops its guard. The octopus
and shark rush in. Shell flies like shrapnel.
But the crab, completely soft, stands
to one side watching. When the frenzy's
done, the shark and octopus, nourished
by nothing, shrink away. The crab,
victorious, turns upon the lamp
and swallows it. Again the creature
grows. Losing all form, mushrooming, it
subsumes the planet, then the universe.

I woke up shaking: like a rocket
at ignition hovers till you
wonder how it's going anywhere.

What is the crab?

                     The crab is terribly
defensive.

          What is the crab?

                          The crab's
a shell, a sham, armored, the thing
it's supposed to be, total response, awkward
rigidity.

          What is the crab?
                          It's
always backing off.

              What is the crab?

I love the taste of it. It tastes like
oceans simmered down. It walks the bottom
filtering whatever filters from
above. Eventually, whole oceans

come to this. The crab is ocean depth
made flesh.

Who's after it?

Parents
I guess. The shark is cruising critically
close, the father, the unblinking
warhead. That tears you up. And then
the family nucleus will offer
to suck back the pieces.

But the lamp?

Power. I stumble on it. I explode
with growth. I step outside myself
and feel the ocean with my own sweet flesh
at last. Then comes despair. I look back
and I'm empty, just a shell. That's when
they attack.

And no one's home.

They
only recognize the thing I was.
Naturally, they're rendered harmless.

But you're not.

Overkill. *I am become
death.* The rage I woke with centered here.
Such softness must be killed.

*I've often
thought your generation felt the bomb
was used on all of them.*

It's true enough
I've never quite grown up. Who wanted
such a world? And who could stand up to

a parent with that weapon? To break
with them risked everything.

                      And fury

was the price.

            And now I'm taking charge.

Let the rocket lift.

            Flesh drops away,
sticks where I step, half-molten wounds
reopening.

          Breathe deep.

               Goddamn it
I want out of this. Out. Out.

               (He cries
a long time.)

        OK, I'm back now,
nauseous a little, bobbing dark
capsule they pluck up and ferry off
through air to some huge carrier.
The hatch springs free. Air rushes in. There's
music, dress whites, bright fine salty air.
I breathe and breathe, can't get enough of it,
then plant feet firmly and emerge.

5

It's midmorning, sunny and autumnal. A scientist sitting in a coffee house peruses a colleague's manuscript on the extinction of species. As the previous two sections delved into human and personal history, here the context shifts to the history of life itself. As the scientist reads, he is interrupted by the sensory world around him and by his own thoughts back over a life of research into whale communication— research lately sponsored by the Defense Department. As he realizes his possible implication in the looming international crisis, he instinctively reaches for a telephone.

Outside the Caffe Dante traffic
streams. Delivery trucks and buses
lumber like herds across a Pleistocene
savannah tawny with wide morning
light. People descend, deliveries
are made. He stirs and spreads the manuscript.
The cosmos in a coffee cup comes
clear, unravels, swirls again toward
tighter mystery. Breath moves upon
the surface of the deep.

if I had
never studied whales.

The holocaust
for dinosaurs occurred time out of mind

the stars went wrong. Asteroids gavelled earth
till numb dust shrouded out all warmth.
During that carboniferous night
green plants which once had shot a hundred feet
through warm, moist air on stalks as tender
as asparagus, collapse to spore.

he's got the subject right at least.

Diplodocus and Brontosaurus,
heaped mountainous, erode away.
Meat-eaters, first bloated, stumble soon
on bones picked clean: in death its prey see
high Tyrannosaurus overthrown.
And under all, nocturnal scavengers,
tunnelling intelligence, small mammals
make way through the reptilian overload
toward their eventual dawn.

                         Steamed milk
pressured toward pure pleasure, the perfect
cappuccino takes off behind him
like a jet, erect.

                    The issue isn't
death. If anything, extinction
proves death's final failure, death again
life's fundamental adaptation to
a changing world, over and again
regrouping as the planet spins out
fluctuating destinies. Imagine
sunlit ocean plankton huddled up
against intensifying salt or
current. Snowballing time accumulates
that sexual pulse in untold zygotes
held bustling as cities, every cell
the self-same individual song.

whales talk
ten thousand miles apart, one saying
to another halfway round the planet
'I am here.'

Light lives in the areca
palm like neon. He looks at it,
his eyes a photosynthesis
equally intense. Dust hums and trembles
in the current.

Nor is knowledge
what went wrong, much as people scapegoat
science. They turn to us their guilt. To think
the brain analogous to fangs
so large they'd choke the feeding sabertooth
explains our missiles only.

twenty
years obscure—pure research—then must be
some shadow network picks up possible
significance. the money starts
to flow.

More like Stegosaurus, its
spiked armament a tail so weighted
it drags back more neurons than the brain
contains. Control is vested furthest from
perception.

no problem anymore
with publication. mainline results
direct to Tennessee.

He studies
the collapse of newsprint columns next

to him, the heads each day absorbing
more black ink.

In blind hope too they turn
to us. In space in time we'll live inside
technology. The way green plants
anticipated atmospheric
oxygen millennia before
the first crustacean crawled aloft, or we
live now within these words, capsuled
reality.

the way an eagle
out of nowhere dives an osprey,
pirating the fish first meant to feed
whole nestfuls.

Deeper escape they want,
a cosmos able to excuse, dispense
pure entropy. They heap their offerings
then pray us prove that easy prophecy
finally the truth.

now they can tell
precisely the coordinates of
every submarine in every ocean.
black pods pregnant with the perfect
defense. who'd argue, all uncertainty
removed.

The woman he's been watching
quickly stands to leave, her dress backlit
like a cathedral window.

In fact
the universe still waits the word
from us, uncertain at its core.

but if

in defense, why such secrecy?

When first
Oppenheimer at Los Alamos
thought his one atom poised to trigger
aerial reactions torching earth
into a star, he hit it close enough.
Such relativity—'everything
changed except our thinking'—leaves us now
profoundly free.

so then suppose
one day empanelled papers in his lap
shout out perfected capability.
the pressures would be too immense.
he'd play the odds, he'd engineer a way
to use the thing.

Biting into light
and ordinary matter we've now found
a density of power able
to darken everything that it
began. The power is not evil.
We got here just by looking. The way
out is the way in. We need only
to see clearly these abstractions, blips,
trajectories mean plain and simple
death, death one breathing person at a time
in magnitudes of billions, those deaths
multiplied time over unseen time
by every possible alignment
of those billion gametes streaming through
each person of those billions now
alive. This much is true. This much is
in our power.

                    He fishes for a dime.
The man at table 21 adjusts
his headset.

          The number at the Times.

6

*At noon a ragtag group of criminals sit around a bar, watching foot-
ball, drinking and planning to knock over a Las Vegas casino. The
leader intimates that the casino's management has put them up to
it, and that if they succeed in starting a big enough fire during the
heist, their percentage of the insurance money could be immense.
An accomplice questions the venture and a fight nearly breaks out.
A background conversation recounts the slaughter of a horse. From
the TV we learn the first real details of the pending crisis.*

       (Stabbing neon reads THE SITUATION
       ROOM. A bar. Polished glasses. Mirrors
       all around. Many points of light. Bottles
       ranged deliberately in what seems
       infinite profusion, many tipped
       with fancy apparatus. Six-foot
       TV screen dominates right side.
       A narrow, horizontal window,
       curtainless, frames passing sidewalk faces.)

               TV

       U.S. forces in Iraq today
       met stiff resistance from Soviet
       advisors. The president is meeting
       with . . .

AL

I say we go in right up through
the front. Take everything at once.
Don't mess around.

TV

And that's the twelve o'clock
and pre-game . . .

LARRY

Now that damn cowboy's
in the White House.

AL

Ed, cut that thing down
and bring me another one.

EARL

Yeah, then what
you going to do, big man? Those places
got more firepower than a fucking
F-15. Look funny and they come
screaming at you from the woodwork.

AL

We takes our chances.

C.W.

He took that horse, see,
and he skewered him. Tongue stuck out pointed
like a knife. He screamed. You ever heard
a horse scream?

AL

      Life, my boy, is all one
big casino. Besides, the point is once
we get the goods, that gives us the excuse
to torch the place. Meet force with force.
That's why we bring the heavy-duty
stuff. That place'll go up like a paper
bag.

EARL

    Like an inferno. Hell, I've seen it
on TV. There's kids in there, you know.
And women. Folks like you and me. Hey—
remember that chic little harem
item you shanghaied last year. She might be
there, you know. What about her?

C.W.

                The bull
just stands there, big balls, careless eyes, tail
raised like smoke.

AL

        You can't get soft.

LARRY

                Look at
that. Look at that mother hit. Sack him.

ED

Bears ain't got shit this year.

AL

                Anyway,
we're homefree in the panic. My friends
assure me the action will be cool
enough for us to operate. Might say
it's in their long-range interests. Hell, boys,
look at this as an advance, just one
hellacious smokescreen.

EARL

                What is it with you?
What are you talking about?

AL

                You are
getting on my nerves. You got no guts.

EARL

I ain't no fucking nazi, that's all.
I don't kill kids and women. I had
enough of that in Nam.

AL

                Call me
that ever again I'll blow your head off.
I fought them bastards for your sake.
Then you run off into the jungle,
come back with your brains defoliated.

ED

Cool it. Cool down. Last fight we had in here
I spent two solid weeks just cleaning up.

Glass everywhere. The mirrors broke.
You'd look in one and think your face
had splintered. And the booze. We all cried.
Six thousand dollars worth of god's best
sacrament. Stank like a butcher's
when it dried. What waste.

LARRY

My. My. My.
Would you look at that. You bet I'd get
mountain spring clean for you mama. Whiter
than white.

C.W.

So everyone looks up, pigeons
pounding at the rafters, trying
to get out. By now his hands are
lacerated. He holds them at weird
angles, you know, hoping to ward off
the pain.

AL

Give us all another round.
The strong stuff. C.W., Dave
don't hear a word you're saying. Everytime
we're getting down to business, he just
gets blitzed into oblivion.
Just doesn't have the stomach for it.

DAVE

Everyday it's getting closer.
Going faster than a roller coaster.

ED

That's ok, he's paying for the whole
shebang.

AL

Get Ronnie off that damn
computer game. We've got to talk
serious logistics.

LARRY

Wait. Wait, here's
the bomb.

EARL

The desert there's incredible.
Every shade of red. And absolutely
empty. A grain of sand might be
exactly where a raindrop cratered it
the year before. Dead silent. Nothing
moves. It's like the moon.

ED

Vegas, man,
the American dream. Everything
you want in one big room there underground—
the food, the women, the machines—
you float your cash and when you hit it
right it all comes back a thousandfold.
We could use a little.

AL

So. The action's
in insurance.

EARL

You're talking blackmail.
Deal me out.

C.W.

There's one bare bulb. The light's
like a barrage of knives. Everything
it hits looks pained. The rest is shades
of darkness.

AL

No one gets left out.

C.W.

She brings the lamp to try to soften things.

7

A man and woman bask in afternoon sunlight and the warm afterglow of making love. They have decided to have a child together. Drifting toward sleep, he enters a half-dream state imbued with mythic imageries of resolution, return, renewal and rebirth. Her television, its volume muted, remains a flickering reminder of events outside.

I turn toward you again studying
the afternoon light through your window
through your hair, feeling how prismatic
we have now become.

*and this is all
there is.*

I love the way you laugh
the way I laugh. I wonder did laughter
start as the only possible summary
of orgasm?

*and now we have embarked
again at last.*
and nothing's changed.

the light streams through your hair the way
the light has always streamed, containing
everything we see. think of light

carrying everything we see all
the way from the sun into your room.
what emptiness has been survived
to bring us this. and what warm welcome
we provide this random incident
of light.

and similarly you now
stream with me.

       there stem harmonics from
your body like a wave of light—long
wave lengthening from some disturbance
clear across an ocean lifting smooth
resolve against this shore.

            the time
it takes us making love, translated
into light, would place us crashing high
up into grainy night.

       but on return
we measure here the universe
or rather it comes down to us, here
meting out what boundaries can be known,
dimensions set, on this our far-flung
pleasure.

       turn then now with open eyes
to meet again

         our small circumference
and circumstance, fear stepping lightly
there as warm wind agitates a summer
woods or surfaces of pools where
children swim, and have, down widening
generations.

>   *we wrestled years with*
> *angels, that old story.*

>   one forgets
> the reasons, forgets their shape. their substance,
> never great, lifts back toward heavens
> one could finally not believe. you're left
> holding the calluses, remembering
> most the hard ground on which everything
> took place, toward which, at last, we now turn
> this embrace.

>   *in island states*

>   *approaching*
> *sleep*

>   *mind and world drift equally*
> *suspended.*

>   images slip and out
> of one another.

>   *like lovers in*
> *and out*

>   *of love.*

>   the wakes of women left
> behind.

>   *there's really nothing left to say.*

> we fought the war for fantasy.
> deceit carried the day.

>   *I only know*
> *we can't go on this way.*

>   she laundered
> me.

*the way waves put their palms against
the shore.*

      then after those salt struggles
lying on the beach exhausted ،
soaking life back from the sand, the coarse
warm grains welcome abrasion.

           *I am
back. we'll make new life.*

         the fog lifts from
familiar headlands, gifts encircling,
air cleared, the final winecup raised,
the weaving and the ocean put to rest,
the stories told and told till dawn can be
contained no longer.

        *feel now warm sun
on closed eyes, round beneath the skin. inside
looking out, the skin the color of
the dawn. that possible. that round.
and this a prayer.*

      'without the sound
your tv's like a fire *black and white.*'

8

A son sits by his father's hospital bed talking to family friends. The father no longer talks, apparently no longer hears, only insists that the television remain on. It has been announced that the President will speak later in the afternoon. The son reflects on his father's military career, his heart disease, and on the distance of their relationship. He then retells two stories exchanged between the men—his father's a war story and his own a hunting tale—in which each reached conclusions inclusive of the other.

No, keep on talking. The sound alone
seems comforting, the fact that we're still here
and talking. The television's
on for that same purpose, dawn to night.
I'm sure it does more good for him than
heart machines and all the rest. Just touch
that set, he throws a fit. Today I know
he wouldn't want to miss, as he would say,
a briefing from the Chief.

                    I never
really saw him as a military
man—more as I see myself sometimes,
an engineer of airfields, or like
every other father that I knew,
a manager of personnel.

I do
remember once when I was five
he came home from some operation
and to pass the time recounted
three years he'd spent in the Pacific.
The high point was a single Japanese
bomber that flew over camp one day.
That's come to be my image of
an air war. It seemed so clean. It is
how that war ended. And now air war's
all we know to talk about. My brother's
memory of Vietnam goes, *They blew him
off my wing. One minute we were
talking on the radio and then
he wasn't there.* When Dad's friends said,
*They died so thick in the Korean
winter the snow turned pink,* I thought they meant
it came out of the air that way.
My uncle went ashore at Normandy
and never mentioned it.

There's such
an eerie distance to it all, like
now the way he sits here out of touch.
I want to shake him. Like the time
I screamed, *You only ever tell me
about death.* You know the way we struggled.
His anger was a different sort I think.
He'd talk about *materiel,*
logistics. The structure was his life.
When things worked well, it was as if the whole
world were remade to answer him—and
he to answer it. The world became
this answerable arrangement, pose
whatever situation might

come up. I mean quite literally those
runways were designed to bring to bear
whole continents on one another.
Here's one thing we do well, he'd say. Just
let some sergeant paint a line wrong
or all the same an offhand general
strike down his pet appropriation,
he'd fume and rage inside himself like
Job against the world not working right.
We used to joke the real idea was get
Dad mad enough, he'd take the Russians
singlehandedly.

         And now his heart.
The doctor came by earlier to talk.
It's blocked again. The bypasses
they did five years ago have gotten
clogged as the original. I can't help
thinking of the engineering
implications—like building a new
circle of freeways every five years
around a city just to keep us
all in motion. The hardening
goes on. No one can account for it:
The center of the body, pumping
life, gathering it back again
from the entire organism,
concentrating and relaxing,
unendingly—this whole community
of cells sustained in oceanic
animation—falters, fails itself.
Its own cells shrivel and we're left
this silent waiting. All for want of
air. If I could put the air in these words
in my father's heart, he'd live.

                              Distance
again. But who am I to talk?
The prodigal son, I fly back here
expecting miracles. We put such faith
in our machines. I think I glimpsed
a little of his present peacefulness
last night when the plane began to
lower. I just leaned back, relaxed, felt
every drop of power, downward
angling of wingflap. Forty minutes
I hung there suspended, feeling
my whole life, all our lives, a part of
something larger, to be trusted.
I haven't felt so rested in months.
Small towns began to hover in
the darkness, then the city rising
like a galaxy we were about
to join. I thought how lovely and how
fragile, all those lights another
human tissue, and more than that, earth's
tissue, earth's consciousness, also
in human hands.

                    He told me something
last time I was down I think he meant
to hold me through my life, to span somehow
our natural distance. His great granddad
died of typhoid in a Union prison
north of Albany. Eight years later,
during Reconstruction, things got so bad
the mother bartered out the son
to work his keep under a butcher.
The boy was ten and beaten daily.
He never did forgive her for it.
He ran away, hid out in a swamp

until a preacher found and raised him.
That was the actual end of civil
war, the solitary peace, for our
family anyway. And that's as far
back as the family history goes. Then
All war is the civil war, my father
said. It seemed the summary of his
reminiscence. It seemed to make him
very sad to tell me that, like something
he would like to pass along, some family
heirloom, had been lost: a thing so crafted
and manhandled that its usefulness
and shape and beauty were completely
gone. I loved him then for giving me
himself instead—and myself, too—
the contradictions and acceptance.
I felt an opening the way sun
strikes down through a clearing in the woods.
I wondered what new stories I might
someday tell my child. And then again
what that grown child would choose to tell
his own. I felt the light redouble like
opposing mirrors glint the infinite.

I told him then the full account
of when my uncle, cousins and myself
went up into the Blue Ridge hunting
deer—some valley they kept to themselves.
I'm twenty. We slept under the stars,
this time of year, Orion rising,
and when dawn came we spread out, each person
his own way. I walked two hours, winding
up a hogback till it merged against
the mountain's flank. Just there a waterfall
dropped clear a hundred feet into

a gorge. I worked a path towards it, shrub
oak and boulders raising sweat now
as the sun gained height. Out on a ledge,
no place to turn, my father's warnings stirred—
Watch out for snakes! Watch where you step!
I lost my balance, slipped full length down
a bulge of rock, hands clawing, catching
at last a crevice. The rifle slithered
out into the air, fell silently
five seconds, fired when it hit.
I fought hard then the urge to follow.
Copperheads came back to me, hundreds
in that crevice, waiting. I felt blood
fanning down my thigh. I got hold of
myself, then pulled up hard, wedged hip and
shoulder into rock, stared pointblank
into the crack. An empty snakeskin
fell back from my breathing. I stood up
easily, regained the ledge, then
made my way down to the water's side.
A point of quartz had caught me where I fell,
slashing a tear along my stomach.
The blood flowed freely now. I felt dumb
anger rise against myself.

       I stripped
and washed the gash there in the frigid
pool below the waterfall, then
shredded shirt and pantslegs, wrapping the wound
securely. The sun shone strong now,
entering my skin, gauzing dry
the water, warming me through. Then pain
rose up like waves of flame venting from
the earth. I fastened on the water,
threading down and down. I took strange

solace in the sound. If I died then
and there, if everything on earth
were dead, this music would go on, streams
muddier perhaps the years it took
to scour soil off, then clear again. I
hung there by that thread all day, the water's
cold thumping and the throbbing in
my wound the same, rifles randomly
connecting in the distance. Towards dark
new strength took hold. I thought, *There's after all*
this healing at the root of things.
I gathered wood and lit a fire.
The others found me then. They never
found the gun.

                  I visited my mother's
grave today. His plot's there too, of course.
This time of year the earth is dying.
Blackbirds pour from the land, the oaks make
fissures in the sky. But these are only
natural continuities. They speak
return. A bit back in the woods
a backhoe waits, metallic yellow
like an insect, invincible,
alone, of human manufacture.

9

Midafternoon. The President's televised speech justifies the ways of war. He reviews the situation; he lists the hardware; he marshals the arguments, worldly and otherworldly. He appeals to pride, justice, freedom, power, camaraderie and martyrdom. He praises, comforts and cajoles. He appears in command. He appears unworried. He appears supremely rational.

Early this morning I received word
that five hundred Soviet advisors
have joined Iraqi forces
in their CONTINUING AND UNPROVOKED
attempts to dislodge the United States
Marine Corps units I have charged
with protecting American oil
interests south of the *Euphrates.*

I have responded by issuing
a CONTINGENCY order for the field
use of small caliber 203
and 155 mm
Howitzer nuclear artillery.

I have also placed on full alert
status the entire strategic
nuclear arsenal of this nation:

1,114
Minuteman and *Titan* ICBMs;
417 B-52
and FB-111 bombers;
744 *Poseidon*,
Trident and *Polaris* SLBMs;
22,000 tactical systems.

Let any enemy consider
well this poised consequence of their own
careless acts. If forced to it we will
mince more than words before this day is done.

Grave as these decisions seem, we have good
reason for them. LET ME SET STRAIGHT
for you the intricacies which led
us to this point:

              First, there are, of course,
PRAGMATIC CONSIDERATIONS. Though
some might argue *Persian Gulf* oil supplies
but six percent of our consumption,
our allies in Europe and Japan
remain vitally dependent on
this source. WE ALONE must buttress friends
in need, or risk deadly isolation
in a world increasingly entwined
and hostile.

              We must recall, too, such
oil's no mere luxury item, feeding
freeways or warming homes, but much more
an ESSENTIAL STRATEGIC RESOURCE
without which this country could sustain

no war of more than ninety days'
duration. Let us heed the lesson
Rommel etched in these same desert sands.

Second, we should turn our attention
to the intangible forces which
sustain a nation. We are A PROUD
PEOPLE wronged by a senseless attack
against our sovereign interests. Certainly
we could no longer COMMAND THE RESPECT
of others—or even a decent
self-respect—were we to leave such low
acts unanswered.

Finally, we stand
before the world A JUST NATION, one
with the power to assert justice
wherever brute strength strives to overwhelm
the rule of law. Surely the ceaseless
Soviet advance these forty years
has been frustrated only through our
rightful vigilance.

Again today
OUR POWER MUST PROVE CREDIBLE
to carry on that larger global
battle for the minds and hearts of men.
The example we provide today
of the UNBENDING DETERMINATION
of free men to preserve the planet's
freedom will not be lost. The evil
of the communist experiment
with this most basic element
of human nature we will in the end
eradicate.

REST ASSURED your nation's
course is justified. The very dangers
of this day prove the correctness of
our military readiness. I trust
this moment to be forge and crucible
of renewed national unity.

I am proud today to serve as your
Commander-in-Chief. I AM PROUD
of the power—as infinitely
destructive as it is minutely
honed—lying here even as I speak
the merest reach away. I AM PROUD
of the American people whose high
ideals and deepest ingenuity
have freed this power. I AM PROUD
that we're the ones chosen to wield such
limitless capacity.

We hope
against hope not to have to use it.
But we must not fear its use. For what
other reason did God entrust this gift
first into the hands of free men?

In simple truth this is a moral
world, a moral universe we live
in. There exist still right and wrong, good
and evil. And we as yet remain
a moral nation, a nation armed
with truth, allied with God, fortified
by an unyielding belief in
the ultimate freedom of mankind
to direct his final destiny.

THERE IS NO HIGHER LAW than this.
We will live free—or die free if we must.

We needn't die. I'm confident
this show of our resolve will turn
around the Russian bear as has proved true
before. But here I turn to you,
the American people, MY UTMOST
PRAISE AND ABSOLUTE FAITH. I draw
my strength today unquestionably
from your own willing, free consent.

                                    In this

new style of war, this war of nerves,
this living-room war, the captive
populations of two continents
face off across uncomprehending
void. We are all in the trenches
this time. We all now face THE SUPREME
SACRIFICE. It heartens me to know how
hardened each of you has gotten to
this final test of human courage.

Should push come to shove, I'm sure also
that each of you has been observing good
basic Civil Defense. National
survival may depend on little
steps taken toward your own survival.
ABOVE ALL ELSE AVOID looking
directly at a nuclear event.

When I leave the air today my image
will be superseded by the stars
and stripes. Throughout the night the flag

will mark those stations keeping you
informed. All other sources of
communication necessarily
will be blackened. Picture therefore this one
image waving proud and clear above
us all. Think then of that earlier
flag, its waves the brilliant coils of
a snake, its plain embroidery
DONT TREAD ON ME. The American
rattlesnake's unique in all the world.
It gives fair warning when disturbed.

This afternoon, the world should note:
We are disturbed. This is our warning.

10

A child has cut school early to scout out an abandoned construction site where friends were supposed to meet him for wargames. The friends, however, have heard the speech at school and gone directly home. The child's anger grows the longer he waits. His thoughts turn gory and macho, then merge in a brief moment of peace with the surrounding autumn woods. Bored, he starts throwing rocks at a hornets' nest.

the kid connects, knocks that baby hard
enough you wake up middle of next week
not knowing which way sunday is.
maybe the school bus didn't make
that lincoln turn for once. god the way
it swerves and screeches everyday, what if
it went? right down the fucking cliff, man,
rolling like a rock, the kids inside
all mashed together, knocked around against
steel grab bars, glass flying everywhere,
seats loose, dresses ripped, guys throwing up.
if it was me I'd time it right and
jump. *probably* they just deserted
me and went to try the dinghy out.
none of them can swim that well. I hope
it sinks. serve them right. *what's going on?*
right after school they said. sure, sure.

what's wrong with those guys. boy, could I surprise
them if I had a firecracker.
get inside that pile of pipes: sound
comes out like a cannon. anyway,
I'll claim it as a fort, stock up on
mud clods, then let them have it, sneak
attack. I'll show them who they're messing
with. what a neat place. they'll still all
want to join up with me. *oh, oh.*
a magazine, a little soggy,
but who's complaining? dynamite!
her tits drip ink. *oh, man. oh, man.*
they're never going to show. I bet their
fucking mothers broke it off. but how
would they know? something's going on.
god this place is quiet. *terry* sure
was weird today, saying right out loud
she dreams of russian missiles coming
in her room. men get out and poke her
full of siphons. they want her blood
because they like how red it is. they
have this storeroom back in russia where
they lock up all the red things in
the world. that's why their missiles are so big,
to haul back all that blood. like my dream
with the garbage truck. every morning
I'm tossed in with all that crud and mashed
and mashed into a brick for building
poison houses with. *forgot* I had these
babies. match rockets. pocket rockets.
donnally really opened up the coop
in science class. *pyromaniacs,*
he says, *everyone of you.* wow, look
at that, a real beaut. must be fifteen feet.
a new world's record for the man.

what's that? this place is getting spooky.
where are those guys? a lot of dirt here,
that's for sure. uuuh, remember that kid
from the projects, he got buried
in a pile like this. could be someone
under here right now for all I know.
if I could start that dozer I could
probably dig up tons of kids. bones
anyway, like on tv. I'd knock
the whole woods down, then show them how to
build a house or two. I wonder what
was supposed to happen here? the gullies
look like probably the way the earth
looked when there wasn't any life—mud
flowers, mud practicing for life. *what's this?*
DANGER. KEEP OUT. WORK STOPPAGE. *due
to the containment memo from HUD
central, model cities branch, current
fluctuating mortgage yields, bond
underwriting services, we must
reluctantly indefinitely
delay.* I'll piss to that. *the foxes
understand.* they know my scent by now.
they'll figure I was staking out
a claim, marking territory. god
they must know everything that happens
here—like where to get good water or
nail a rabbit, jump him, tear the thing
apart. it's how they stay alive.
every move I make I leave them secret
messages. I'm glad they're on my side.
sometimes they even show themselves like
talking back. this time of year the whole
woods feel like fur. like mom's old stole before
the wreck. *you'd think* in all this dirt

there'd be an arrowhead or fossil.
nothing but rocks. the right size though to reach
the hornets' nest. now that would be a show
and tell. donnally would love it. I'd hold
it up, *proud headhunter back from
amazon.* they handle strange, light like
a paper globe. *not even close.* I'll
never hit the thing. dumb hornets don't
even know I'm here. it's neat though how
they buzz the place like jets around
a carrier, or satellites, maybe
electrons—thousands of them. armed to
the hilt to hold the fort. *get ready*
for the creek, you hit those suckers
the whole woods explodes, pulsar force shield
snapped in place, disintegrating foreign
flesh, only escape you turn yourself
like stone or water, something they
accept. like people just by thinking
right can reach barehanded honey out
of hives, much as they want, the queen there
at the center with her grubs left
churning more and more. I'll tell them
what I saw. that should be good enough.

11

Waiting for missiles, a man makes a late night journal entry. He recounts the details noticed as he walked the city after the speech. He records his present circumstance, writing, waiting. He commits himself to four practical steps to planetary longevity. Then facing up to and letting in his fear, he experiences himself fully a part of the planet's physical reality; he resolves to represent and protect that reality as his own true constituency. He applies this newfound politic-poetic to a further recounting of the day, including his upstate leave-taking of wife and child for the city.

thursday, october 27.
left work following the speech today.
walked home. traffic absolutely jammed.
sidewalks strangely empty. to walk felt
good—free and under my own power.
late fall light, fall air, fall dust up off
the concrete. expansive. red-veined maple
leaf at rest on concrete. the air
emptying of light. imagine one
more time such sure erasure of each
scene and detail passed—today indented
cornices on 22nd
street, fine neon just next door—gone quick
as blinking. a blinding flash. this my
military exercise. I close
my eyes.

        men roofing. the stench of tar
from that small hell they carry with them
steeps the neighborhood.

                        near midnight now.
bituminous. they've cut our power off.
I'm writing this by kerosene,
the one antique I own. imagine.
do they think the missiles cannot see?
and then what? turn around? call it a night?
who are these vandals tampering with me—
in my name threatening to brush away
as if we were a globe of gnats
this planet's consciousness? light shivers
on walled darkness like a shallow sea
pressed down to oil. scared ghost of hope.

principles of hope should this night pass:

1. end development and deployment
   of these weapons. mutually reduce
   numbers to coincide with sane
   military and national interests.

2. reinvest weapons expenditures
   in human and planetary
   development, equalizing
   resources and living expectations.

3. move toward planetary institutions
   to supersede the nation-state
   in matters of security and
   resource allocation. once in place
   eradicate nuclear stockpiles.

4. delve psychological, social and
   biological roots of conflict.

went up earlier to meet head-on
incoming missiles. back flat against
the deck. night an isotope entering
my bones, worn carcass crawling with
its stars.

      each meteor rains shaking
cold deteriorating terror.

                  pound
fists raw against ungiving wood.

                       let
enter now. let liquid flesh reshape
to this dark influence, to contours,
waves, wide fluencies, as if my surface
were the planet's, back flat against,
this instant giving way into all
others.

      now, new strength regathering,
with my own hands to wrestle down
this steel convergence:

            beat back boundaries
and here and now convene new governance
of things,

      each particle and surface
voicing self toward what unending ends
such universal suffrage

            determines.

think back the history of the morning.
outside dry cleaners, voice the smelt flame
pressed on city air. cackling eggs fried
up. cut grass (sweet maintenance). passing
women waked fresh from showers.

                                        retouch
limbs fingering fall light, handing it
down to earth. light held in fold and stitch
of oscillating wool. light strobing
marble till it lives again as first
in calcium precipitated
from flecked ocean surface.

                              enter
corner grocery lists. roll over grape
on tongue, burst wide open as the day
this small globe, test and inventory,
arrive at just accounts.

                        diversely
as the street administers itself
let live the earth.

                    think back again piles
being pounded as new buildings
shoulder morning sky.

                        leavetaking like
a hundred other mornings, millions
really. hard though to retrieve, gesture
dissolving into gesture. nothing
holds.

                she holds the child against one hip,
whole body balanced with

                              the weight. he
pulls back, buries face into her
softness, then reaches

                        out, an orchestrating
finger toward the world, toward me, tentative,
enduring, as the air.

                rest now this
night, silent and soluble, from which
like crystal, city now descends
to earth again, long breath let go.

slow eggshell dawn I'll hunker down on
like grenade until the way is clear.

12

*Dawn arrives. A man who has been riding the Staten Island ferry
all night gets off and walks through Battery Park. Images of the entire
country course through him, peaceful and connecting. Fear comes
and goes. He meets someone. He calls home. The city comes alive
another day.*

He moves across the water, back and
forth, his mind drifting, emptying
the night.

        The city, laid flat, floats
in front of him, breathing peacefully
a deep dream.

           Window by window, lights
come on, patterning like a computer
printout infinite arrangements of
a theme.

         The ferry had seemed something
safe to do. Any repetition
mimics sanity. He'd lost count of
the passages. The early neon
nervous smack of waves had given way
to simple blackness, and now this calm.

Now overhead the dawn's mitosis
starts its lengthy separations.

He steps ashore, the feel of firm
earth rising into him again.

                    Along
the Battery the oaks raise their still
tracery against the sky, broken
erratically by small birds making
notes on the migration south.

                    Leaning
his full weight against the rail, he looks
again into the water. His mind
dissolves, goes out with the waves, returns
molecular in comprehension
of the unity of oceans:
that this water touches every coast.
He smiles.

          The jetsam and the oil
suddenly were friendly, prismatic
in possibility.

          He smiles
remembering the strength of the Pacific
raising its slow swells against the edge
of continent, mountain for mountain,
and soft hills pulsing inland,

                    and the storms,
great spiral shells of air progressing
off Siberia, the Humboldt
current, moistening interior
valleys,

        imprinting dry arroyos
through a quarter of the country
differently each spring,

              and waves in grain
driven by that same wind, rising with
moisture also, then barged down

                the larger
river systems, past still southern swamp
and out into the Gulf, perhaps
returning to that Asian heartland.

Up this river now in this still dawn
he pictures high cathedral elms
detailing in twig and root and
periodic foliage these branching
unities.

        It was as if he held
a stack of postcards, sent and kept
on impulse. On the back of each were words
from people whom he loved and who were
far away, but well and having
a good time.

           Behind him, startled by
the stillness, he wheels to face in sudden
cold light the glass and concrete city.
Sickening, he wonders if this all
could be illusion, the creation
of a mind point blank with death. After all,
he reasons, this close no one would know
the instant of the actual war.
He might have been who knew how long
obliterated and this his own

empty afterlife, a tomb city
he might search eternally, fearing
and despairing, for another soul.

Far down the granite seawall a black speck
grows into a man, opening
inside him now a different void. Again
he glances rapidly about for
other people, thinking how careless
this of all nights left him. There are none.
He braces, watches the approach.

Good, my man, good morning to you.
And a blinding smile.

                                 Hell of a night.

Hell of a night for sure.

                         He turns now
quickly, memory flooding back.

                           *Say,
you don't have a dime? I need to call
someone real bad. Last night, I didn't
think. Thanks. Thanks.*

                     Out of the sky in soft
formation rock doves having found
in dawn's gray hour some outland farmer's field
return now; wings outstretched and wheeling
round like sickle moons they home.

                        Cab unfurls
a corner, dances over empty
lanes. Bus more straightforward. Sound starts now
to build its city.

Now the ferry,
back again and full.

Streets fill. He walks
on liquid streets, joins in, the faces
like those filing through some liberation
newsreel grim and joyous in ongoing
disbelief.

He finds himself returning
back and forth along the Battery,
his own patrol.

Behind him now,
light gathering its strength, the city
rises pearled against the pending day.

William Carney was born on a Nebraska Air Force base in 1948. His poetry has won two American Academy of Poets prizes and a Hutchinson Fellowship at Williams College. The author of several New England town plans, he is a landscape architect who now lives and practices in San Francisco.